Christmas 2025

Dear Mom,

When I think [illegible] en,

I think of you. [illegible]

[illegible]

IN THEIR OWN WORDS

Pioneer Women of Faith

Many thanks to the Daughters of Utah Pioneers and to Jolene S. Allphin and Andrew D. Olsen, without whose contributions this book could not have happened.

Note: Spelling and punctuation in historical accounts shared in this volume have been modernized; accounts have been used with permission.

All art by Sandra Rast and Julie Rogers. For print information on Sandra's art, please visit sandrarast.com. For print information on Julie's art, please visit julierogersart.com. Black-and-white historical photos from familysearch.org
Design by Christina Marcano © 2025 by Covenant Communications, Inc.
Published by Covenant Communications, Inc.
American Fork, Utah

Printed in China
First Printing: March 2025

32 31 30 29 28 27 26 25 10 9 8 7 6 5 4 3 2 1

ISBN 978-1-52442-789-4

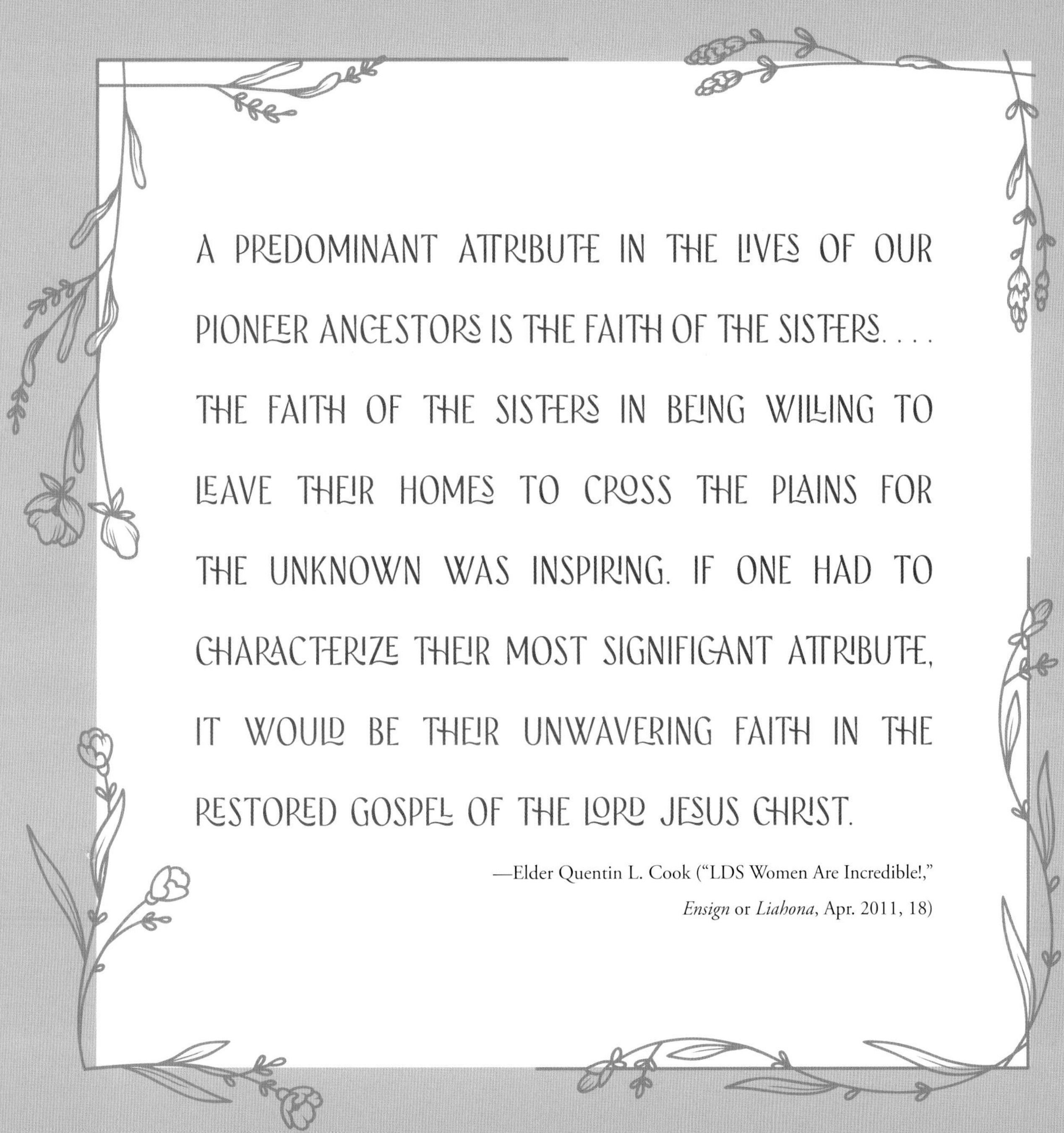

A PREDOMINANT ATTRIBUTE IN THE LIVES OF OUR PIONEER ANCESTORS IS THE FAITH OF THE SISTERS. . . . THE FAITH OF THE SISTERS IN BEING WILLING TO LEAVE THEIR HOMES TO CROSS THE PLAINS FOR THE UNKNOWN WAS INSPIRING. IF ONE HAD TO CHARACTERIZE THEIR MOST SIGNIFICANT ATTRIBUTE, IT WOULD BE THEIR UNWAVERING FAITH IN THE RESTORED GOSPEL OF THE LORD JESUS CHRIST.

—Elder Quentin L. Cook ("LDS Women Are Incredible!," *Ensign* or *Liahona*, Apr. 2011, 18)

When we reached the Black Hills, we had a rough experience. The roads were rocky, broken, and difficult to travel. Frequently carts were broken down and much delay [was] caused by the needed repairs.

In crossing the Platte River, some of the men carried a number of the women on their backs or in their arms across the stream, while others of the women tied up their skirts and waded through like [the] heroines that they were. My husband also attempted to ford the stream, but he had only gone a short distance when he reached a sand bar in the river on which he sank down through weakness and exhaustion. My sister, Mary Horrocks Leavitt, waded through the water to his assistance. She raised him up to his feet. Shortly afterward, a man

"Others of the women tied up their skirts and waded through [the Platte River] like [the] heroines they were."

came along on horseback and conveyed him to the other side of the river, placed him on the bank, and left him there. My sister then helped me to pull my cart with my three children and other matters on it. We had scarcely crossed the river when we were visited with a tremendous storm of snow, hail, sand, and fierce winds. It was a terrible storm from which both the people and teams suffered. After crossing the river, my husband was put on a handcart and hauled into camp; and indeed after that time he was unable to walk and consequently provision had to be made for him to ride in a wagon. As soon as we reached camp, I prepared some refreshments and placed him to rest for the night. From this time my worst experience commenced. The company had now become greatly reduced in strength, the teams as well as the people. The teams

had become so weak that the luggage was reduced to ten pounds per head for adults and five pounds for children under eight years. And although the weather was severe, a great deal of bedding and clothing had to be destroyed—burned—as it could not be carried along. This occurrence very much increased the suffering of the company, men, women, and children alike.

On the 20th of October we traveled, or almost wallowed, for about ten miles through the snow. At night, weary and worn out, we camped near the Platte River, where we soon left it for the Sweetwater. We were visited with three days more snow. The animals and emigrants were almost completely exhausted. We remained in camp

several days to gain strength. About the 25th of October, I think it was—I cannot remember the exact date—we reached camp about sundown. My husband had for several days previous been much worse. He was still sinking, and his condition became more serious. As soon as possible, after reaching camp, I prepared a little of such scant articles of food as we then had. He tried to eat but failed. He had not the strength to swallow. I put him to bed as quickly as I could. He seemed to rest easy and fell asleep. About nine o'clock, I retired. Bedding had become very scarce, so I did not disrobe. I slept until, as it appeared to me, about midnight. It was extremely cold. The weather was bitter. I listened to hear if my husband breathed—he lay so still. I could not hear him. I became alarmed. I put my hand on his body, when, to my horror, I discovered that my worst fears were confirmed. My husband was dead. He was cold and stiff—rigid in the arms of death. It was a bitter freezing night and the elements had sealed up his mortal frame. I called for help to the other inmates of the tent. They could render me no aid, and there was no alternative but to remain alone by the side of the corpse till morning. . . . There was nothing with which to produce a light or kindle a fire. Of course I could not sleep. I could only watch, wait, and pray for the dawn. But oh, how those dreary hours drew their tedious length along. When daylight came, some of the male part of the company prepared the body for burial. And oh, such burial and funeral service. They did not remove his clothing—he had but little. They wrapped him in a blanket and placed him in a pile with thirteen others who had died, and then covered him up in the snow. The ground was frozen so hard that they could not dig a grave.

I will not attempt to describe my feeling at finding myself thus left a widow with three children under such excruciating circumstances. I cannot do it. But I believe the Recording Angel has inscribed it in the archives above, and that my sufferings for the gospel's sake will be sanctified unto me for my good. My sister was the only relative I had to whom I could look for assistance in this trying ordeal, and she was sick. . . .

The Vault of Heaven © Julie Rogers

I could therefore appeal to the Lord alone—He who had promised to be a husband to the widow and a father to the fatherless. I appealed to Him, and He came to my aid.

A few days after the death of my husband, the male members of the company had become reduced in number by death, and those who remained were so weak and emaciated by sickness that on reaching the camping place at night, there were not sufficient men with strength enough to raise the poles and pitch the tents. The result was that we camped out with nothing but the vault of heaven for a roof and the stars for companions. The snow lay several inches deep upon the ground. The night was bitterly cold. I sat down on a rock with one child in my lap and one on each side of me. In that condition I remained until morning. . . .

It will be readily perceived that under such adverse circumstances I had become despondent. I was six or seven thousand miles from my native land, in a wild rocky mountain country, in a destitute condition, the ground covered with snow, the waters covered with ice, and I with three fatherless children with scarcely anything to protect them from the merciless storms. When I retired to bed that night, being the 27th of October, I had a stunning revelation. In my dream, my husband stood by me and said; "Cheer up, Elizabeth, deliverance is at hand."

The dream was fulfilled, for the next day (October 28, 1856) Joseph A. Young, Daniel Jones, and Abel Garr galloped unexpectedly into camp, amid tears and cheers and smiles and laughter of the emigrants. These three men were the first of the most advanced relief company sent out from Salt Lake City to meet the belated emigrants. Though the sufferings after that still continued, yet the worst was over and the survivors of that ill-fated handcart company arrived in Salt Lake City November 30, 1856. ***I have a desire to leave a record of those scenes and events through which I have passed that my children, down to my latest posterity, may read what their ancestors were willing to suffer, and did suffer, patiently for the gospel's sake.*** And I wish them to understand, too, that what I now word is the history of hundreds of others who have passed through like scenes for the same cause. I also desire them to know that it was in obedience to the commands of the true and living God, and with the assurance of an eternal reward—an exaltation in his kingdom—that we suffered these things. I hope, too, that it will inspire my posterity with fortitude to stand firm and faithful to the truth, and be willing to suffer and sacrifice all things they may be required to pass through for the sake of the kingdom of God.

—Elizabeth Horrocks Jackson Kingsford, emigrated from England in 1856 aboard the *Horizon*, joined the Martin handcart company at Iowa City (Andrew Jenson, comp., *Latter-day Saint Biographical Encyclopedia*, vol. 2 [[Salt Lake City: Andrew Jenson Company and Deseret News, 1914], 528–531; "Leaves from the Life of Elizabeth Horrocks Jackson Kingsford," familysearch.org; https://www.tellmystorytoo.com/member_pdfs/elizabeth-horrocks-jackson_1133_646.pdf)

I can truthfully say that **we never felt to murmur at the hardships** we were passing through.

—Patience Loader, Martin handcart company (Patience Loader Rozsa Archer, as cited in *Recollections of Past Days: The Autobiography of Patience Loader Rozsa Archer*, ed. Sandra Ailey Petree [Logan, UT: Utah State University Press, 2006], 86, https://digitalcommons.usu.edu/cgi/viewcontent.cgi?article=1036&context=usupress_pubs)

During the time we were waiting, a good brother came to our campfire. . . . He asked Mother if she had no husband. She told [him] her husband had died two months ago and he was buried on the plains. He had been standing with his hands behind him. Then he handed us a nice piece of beef to cook for our supper. He left us and came back with a beef bone. He said, "Here is a bone to make you some supper, and . . . don't quarrel over it." We felt surprised that he should think we would ever quarrel over our food. Mother said, "Oh brother, we never quarrel over having short rations, but we feel very thankful to you for giving us this meat, for we had not got any meat, neither did we expect to have any."

—Patience Loader, emigrated from England aboard the *John J. Boyd* before joining the Martin handcart company (Patience Loader Rozsa Archer, as cited in *Recollections of Past Days: The Autobiography of Patience Loader Rozsa Archer*, ed. Sandra Ailey Petree [Logan, UT: Utah State University Press, 2006], 81, https://digitalcommons.usu.edu/cgi/viewcontent.cgi?article=1036&context=usupress_pubs; see also Stewart E. Glazier and Robert S. Clark, eds., *Journal of the Trail* [Salt Lake City, Utah: The Church of Jesus Christ of Latter-day Saints, 2007; first published 1997], 91–92)

Our dear mother said she had never seen her family want for bread, but said the Lord would provide. About midnight that night, all the camp had retired, and we were awakened with a noise. . . . To our great surprise, the noise was caused by the teamsters of a relief team, and some of the camp shouted for joy. . . . They were loaded with all kinds of provisions: flour, bread, butter, meat of all kinds, but all frozen so hard. . . . I remember we had to cut everything with the hatchet, ***but oh how thankful we all were that the Lord had answered our prayers and saved us all from starvation.***

—Elizabeth White, emigrated from England aboard the *Horizon* before joining the Hunt wagon company (Autobiography of Elizabeth White Stewart, written by herself at the age of seventy-six years, familysearch.org)

Silent Prayer © Sandra Rast

Many cruel and painful things happening, the dying and dear ones all around us, poor souls, would sit down by the roadside and would never move again until carried into camp on handcarts by someone. It is a wonder any of us lived through it. My husband's health still failing, a young woman by the name of Caroline Marchant assisted me with the cart. . . . Not far from here [Devil's Gate], the captain called us together to tell us we must lay our bodies down. Were we willing to do so for the gospel's sake? Many poor half-starved men shouted with what remaining strength they had, "Aye." But mothers could not say that and were quiet. We went back to our tents. Food would have suited us then. My faith was in my Heavenly Father. I never lost that faith in Him. It is as sweet today to trust, and my prayer is may I always trust Him. He is a friend that has never failed.

—Elizabeth Sermon, emigrated from England aboard the *Caravan* before joining the Martin handcart company (Glazier and Clark, *Journal of the Trail*, 104).

After consuming their last pound of flour days before, it was here that Jens and Elsie gained a victory over almost certain death through their great physical strength, indomitable courage, and unconquerable spirits. Their strength had carried them beyond the endurance of the other four men in their camp who had succumbed to the snow, cold, starvation and exhaustion, and had been buried in shallow graves under the snow [at Rock Creek]. Also buried was Jens and Elsie's twelve-year-old son, Neils, and the Mortensen girl [Bodil Mortenson]. The end appeared to be near and certain for Jens. His feet became so frozen he could not walk another step, which caused his right foot to be at right angles the rest of his life. At this point, Jens said to Elsie, "Leave me by the trail in the snow to die, and you go ahead and try to keep up with the company

and save your life." If you believe men have a monopoly on strength and courage, then pay heed to Elsie's immortal words when she said, "Ride. I can't leave you; I can pull the cart." Jens had to suffer the humiliation of riding while Elsie pulled like an ox. He later said when describing this ordeal, "No person can describe it, nor could it be comprehended or understood by any human living in this life, but those who were called to pass through it."

—Descendant Jay P. Nielson, about Jens and Elsie Nielson, who emigrated from Denmark aboard the *Thornton*, then joined the Willie handcart company (Glazier and Clark, *Journal of the Trail*, 166)

"Our mother was a martyr for the truth. I thought of her words, 'Polly, I want to go to Zion while my children are small, so they can be raised in the gospel of Christ, for I know this is the true Church.'"

—Mary Goble Pay, emigrated from England aboard the *Horizon* before joining the Hunt and Hodgett wagon companies (Mary Goble Pay, autobiographical sketch, 1896–1909, Church History Library, Salt Lake City; Selections from the Autobiography of Mary Goble Pay, BYU Religious Studies Center, https://rsc.byu.edu/rescued/selections-autobiography-mary-goble-pay)

There was no fear in my heart, for I knew we were in the hands of God and He would do all things right. Oh! How kind and merciful is our Father in Heaven. He watches

over us all the day long, and when the night comes, He is still our guard. Even the great God that holds the reins of government over all His vast dominion condescends to watch over us poor, weak, frail mortals.

—Sarah Sturtevant Leavitt, emigrated from England, then joined the Milo Andrus wagon company in 1850 ("History of Sarah Studevant Leavitt," copied from her journal by Juanita Leavitt Pulsipher, 1919, familysearch.org)

Mother says, "Come, girls, this will not do. I believe I will have to dance to you and try to make you feel better." Poor dear Mother, she started to sing and dance to us, and she slipped down as the snow was frozen. And in a moment we [were] all up to help our

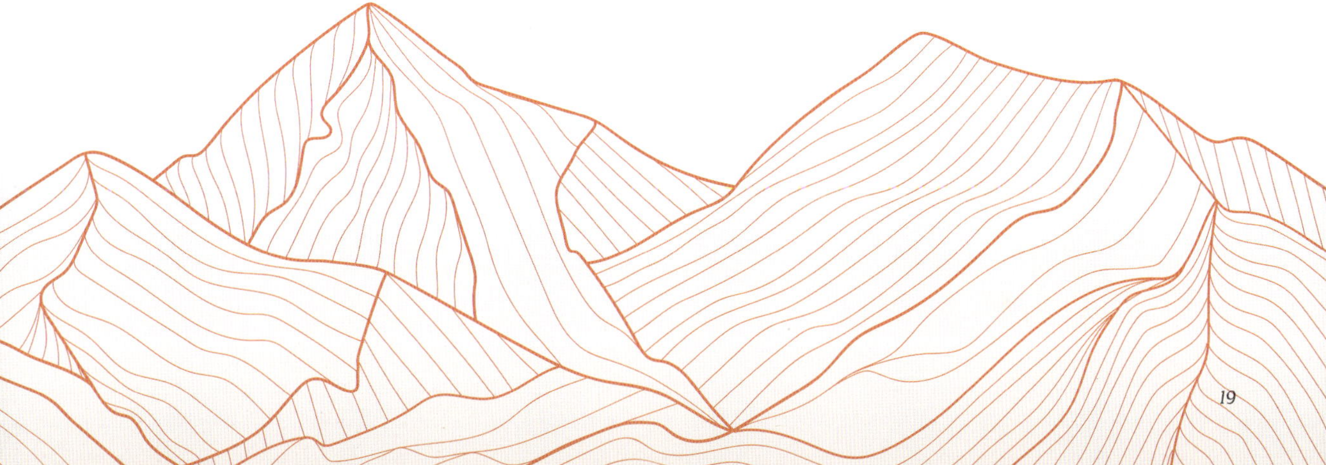

dear Mother up, for we [were] afraid she was hurt. She laughed and said, "I thought I could soon make you all jump up if I danced to you." Then we found that she fell down purposely, for she knew we would all get up to see if she was hurt. She said that she was afraid her girls [were] going to give out and get discouraged, and she said that would never do to give up. . . .

Some time in the afternoon a strange man appeared to me. . . . He came and looked in my face. He said, "Are you Patience?" I said, "Yes." He said . . . "I thought it was you. Travel on, there is help for you. You will come to a good place. There is plenty." With this he was gone. He disappeared. I looked but never saw where he went. This seemed very strange to me. I took this as someone sent to encourage us and give us strength.

—Patience Loader, emigrated from England aboard the *John J. Boyd* before joining the Martin handcart company (Patience Loader Rozsa Archer, *Recollections of Past Days: The Autobiography of Patience Loader Rozsa Archer*, ed. Sandra Ailey Petree [Logan, UT: Utah State University Press, 2006] 79, 87)

I have no memory of my father, as before my birth he set sail for the Canadian borders. He had visited with his parents [in Canada] and was on his way to the United States to investigate the feasibility of bringing his family to America or Canada. His parents notified mother about the news that he was lost at sea. His name was neither on the list of those saved [nor] those lost. You . . . can well imagine it was no easy thing for mother to make a living for a family of five, three boys and two girls. Necessarily, I was brought up in the strictest economy. The Mormon Elders visited us from time to time as preparations were going on for our departure to the great Rocky Mountains and the bosom of the Church. To this end, my mother was bending every effort to prepare herself and family to emigrate. I have often marveled at the faith and courage of my mother in undertaking to forsake her all to be with the Saints. . . .

The source of cheerfulness is hope. The supply of cheerfulness comes through faith. We can do a great deal if we are living as we should. Then we can go to our Heavenly Father in all confidence knowing that he answers prayers. . . .

Did you ever know how many of us complain unthinkingly? We complain about the weather. We complain about the seasons. It is either too hot or too cold. Did it ever occur to you that our Father in Heaven rules over all and does all things well. This reminds me of a lady who stayed overnight with me. She had to go by team eight miles before she got her train. It was just pouring down rain that morning. As she was going, I said I was sorry it was such a bad morning. Think how I felt, me being a Latter-day Saint and she a non-Mormon, when she said, "The Lord does everything well." I commenced to think how ungrateful I was of the Lord's blessings. I started right then trying to be more conscious of the Lord's blessings by trying to be more grateful, cheerful and uncomplaining.

—Agnes Caldwell, emigrated from Scotland aboard the *Thornton* before joining the Willie handcart company (Jolene Allphin, *Tell My Story, Too*, 8)

From New York we traveled by rail and by way of Lake Erie to the camping grounds in the neighborhood of Iowa City; there we were obliged to wait 'til the companies were

ready to start, and surely if we had been natural or unnatural curiosities, we could not have been commented on or stared at any more by the people surrounding us. "Mormon men, women, and children, and worse, a lot of young girls, bound for Salt Lake and going to pull 'handcarts!' Shocking!" Yet, for the potent reason that no other way seemed open, and on the principle [of] "descending below all things," I made up my mind to pull a handcart. All the way to Zion, a foot journey from Iowa to Utah, and pull our luggage, think of it!

Anonymous letters and warnings from sympathizing outsiders were mysteriously conveyed to us, setting forth the hardships and impossibilities of such a journey and offering us inducements to stay. Many who started out with us backed out in a few days. . . . I remember asking myself (footsore and weary with the first week of walking and

EMILY LATER WROTE THE HYMN "AS SISTERS IN ZION."

working) if it was possible for me, faith or no faith, to walk twelve hundred miles further. The flesh certainly was weak, but the spirit was willing. I set down my foot that I would try, and by the blessing of God I pulled a handcart a thousand miles and never rode one step. Some thrilling scenes I could relate incident to that journey, and must forbear for want of space. Suffice it to say that after a long and wearisome journey, being entirely out of provisions, we halted for want of strength to proceed, and never should I have beheld (with mortal eyes) "the city of the Saints" had not the compassionate people of Utah sent out a number of brave-hearted brethren with food and clothing to our relief. May they all be everlastingly blessed.

—Emily Hill Woodmansee, emigrated from England aboard the *Thornton*, then joined the Willie handcart company (Autobiography of Emily Hill Woodmansee, Leonard J. Arrington Historical Archives, Special Collections, Utah State University, Logan, Utah, as cited in Jolene S. Allphin, *Tell My Story, Too*, 41; see also *Tales of Triumph*, vol. 6, 184)

Sister's in Zion © Julie Rogers

As sisters in Zion, we'll all work together;

The blessings of God on our labors we'll seek.

We'll build up his kingdom with earnest endeavor;

We'll comfort the weary and strengthen the weak.

—Text by Emily H. Woodmansee, "As Sisters in Zion" (*Hymns*, no. 309)

One evening just as the sun had sunken out of sight, little three-year-old Mary was missing. While her mother was busy with the care of the baby she, Mary Ellen, had slipped out of sight. Mother called, and Father called, "Mary, Mary." There was no answer except they thought they heard a faint cry . . . Mrs. Melling in her excitement thrust the baby into its father's arms and ran to locate the direction of the sound. Going around a clump of brush she spied a trail in the deep grass where something had been dragged. She followed and the sound of childish cries came clearer. She ran faster and kept the trail which led her to a den of lions, mountain lions. There the old mother lion was just dropping little Mary, whom she had carried by her clothes, in front of her family of baby lions, presenting them with little Mary for their evening meal. The old mother lion and her pretty kittens stood in awe while Mrs. Melling apparently was wading into the jaws of death, to snatch her child to safety. All that happened; the old mother lion growled fiercely, showing her teeth, but she never moved to harm Mrs. Melling. Little Mary had not been bitten by the lion lady but was scratched some from being dragged through the brush and grass!*

—about Ellen Knowles Melling Salisbury (*Tales of Triumph*, vol. 6, 188)

**Although this story is from a pioneer who crossed the plains and then was on her way with her family back to St. Louis when this event occurred, it illustrates the tenacity of pioneer women.*

Our journey was like all such journeys—it had its pleasant side, and its unpleasant side. When the sun was shining and the roads were good, we trotted along feeling that we would soon be at our destination, but when the rain poured down and the roads were so bad that we could not travel—then that was the other side.

—Margaret Gay Judd Clawson, Allen Taylor wagon company (Margaret Gay Judd Clawson. Reminiscences, holograph, Church Archives. Manuscript is also filed in the Library of Congress, Washington, D.C.; see also "Rambling Reminiscences of Margaret Gay Judd Clawson," The Relief Society Magazine, vol. 6, no. 5 [May 1919], 251–62, 317–27, 391–400, 474–79, 505–9)

With all our trials, our weary traveling, burying our dear ones, . . . we have never once felt to murmur or complain or regret the steps we have taken.

—Eliza Reeder Hurren, Willie handcart company (Allphin, *Tell My Story, Too*, 47)

After three and one-half months walking over a hot desert, up the rugged hills, and down the hills and canyons, we finally came out of Emigration Canyon, dirty and ragged. When I saw my mother looking over this valley with the tears streaming down her pale cheeks, she made this remark: "Is this Zion, and are we at the end of this long, weary journey?" Of course to me as a child, this had been a delightful pleasure jaunt, and I remember it only as fun. We children would run along as happy as could be. My older sisters used to make rag dolls as they walked along for us little children to play with. But to my mother, this long, hot journey with all of us ragged and footsore at the end and the arrival in the valley of desert and sagebrush must have been a heartbreaking contrast to the beautiful home she had left in Sweden. But **to me and to my mother, the gospel had been worth all it had cost.**

—Alma Elizabeth Mineer Felt, emigrated from Sweden aboard the *Monarch of the Sea*, then joined the John Riggs Murdock wagon company in 1861 (Alma Elizabeth Mineer Felt, Journal, in *An Enduring Legacy*, vol. 7 [Salt Lake City: Daughters of Utah Pioneers, 1984], 200)

Until We Meet Again © Sandra Rast

THE GOSPEL HAD BEEN WORTH ALL IT HAD COST

The day we left Nauvoo, we had not had flour for weeks. Father purchased a little white flour and Mother made some light bread. We children were so anxious to eat we would keep asking how long it would be until we could eat. ***Our, dear patient mother did not get angry with us as most mothers do, but when we did get to eat, what a feast it was:*** *white bread and milk from old Muley! Never have I had such a dinner.*

—Lucina Mecham Boren, Appleton M. Harmon wagon company (Autobiography of Lucina Mecham Boren, comps., Minerva Boren Marriotti and Wilford Wells Boren, FamilySearch Library, 6; Susan Arrington Madsen, *I Walked to Zion: True Stories of Young Pioneers on the Mormon Trail* [Salt Lake City: Deseret Book, 1994], 118)

A very remarkable thing happened while we were at the Platte River. One of the oxen, used to pull the wagons, died. Brother Ellsworth asked the brethren what could be done. Should we place a cow in the team? One brother said. "Look, Brother Ellsworth, at that steer on the hill." There stood a large fat steer looking at us. ***Brother Ellsworth said that the Lord had provided the animal that we may move on to the mountains.*** *The animal worked as well as the others. When we were within two days of Salt Lake City, we met some wagons sent with provisions and to help us the remainder of the way. The next morning, when gathering the animals, that steer was gone. After hunting for him for several hours, Brother Ellsworth said, "The Lord loaned him to us as long as we needed him."*

—Mary Ann Jones Ellsworth, emigrated from England, then joined the Edmund Ellsworth handcart company in 1856 (Mary Ann Jones Ellsworth file, Daughters of the Utah Pioneers history file; see also *Tales of Triumph*, vol. 6, 223)

I think I shall never forget that long, lonely day after leaving Nauvoo, Illinois, waiting on that vast, undulating prairie that stretched as far as the eye could reach, covered with grass and flowers. It must have been a lovely scene that bright spring morning, but I hardly think it was properly appreciated by the little band who were so bravely leaving home, friends, country, and kindred to take their toilsome march across the Rocky Mountains.

The oxen were detached from the wagons and feeding lazily among the green grass, knowing nothing of the future that lay before them, or that before many months their bones would, many of them, whiten on the desert sands. My childish heart knew as little as they of the hardship that lay before us. My pale, delicate mother watched the teams while my father busied himself assisting or counseling those who were starting out. No doubt her heart failed her on that long, weary day as she sat in the bright spring sunshine, watching the shadows and thinking of all she was leaving behind and wondering what the future held in store for her.

—Mary Jane Mount Tanner, Abraham O. Smoot/George B. Wallace wagon company (Mary Jane Mount Tanner, Reminiscences and Diary, Church History Library, Salt Lake City, as cited in Susan Arrington Madsen, *I Walked to Zion: True Stories of Young Pioneers on the Mormon Trail*, 112)

Two years later, Barzilla and Matthew crossed the plains with their three children and the Aaron Johnson Company. Cholera broke out in the camp and several people died. As soon as death occurred, Johnson ordered a grave dug and the deceased buried, bed and all. Barzilla, seeing this, remarked, "I never will allow any of my people buried like that." The next morning, her husband fell across the wagon tongue, apparently dead from cholera. Captain Johnson ordered a grave dug and him put in it. Barzilla said, "No, you need not bother yourselves. I'll see to it myself." Barzilla was told she would be left alone with his body. Her reply was, "Drive on!" With her parents in the next wagon, her mother took one of her chickens. Ryan's neck ripped it open and place it in the kettle, feathers and all. As soon as it began to boil, they pried Matthew's mouth open with a spoon handle, poured some soup down him and he revived shortly thereafter. They soon overtook the wagon train, as it was starting out on the trail in the afternoon.

—about Barzilla Guyman (Guymon) Caldwell, Aaron Johnson wagon company (Golden V. Adams, Jr. "Barzilla Guymon Caldwell," *Daughters of the Utah Pioneers History Collection*; see also *Tales of Triumph*, vol. 6, 264)

Bread of Life © Julie Rogers

Because of her natural merry disposition, she [Elizabeth Pixton] was often sent among the groups at night after camp was made to cheer up the more disheartened with her jokes and stories. It was said of her that she would be telling jokes on her deathbed. Her good humor was tempered by a chief characteristic of hers which was to speak pointedly, even bluntly. One did not have to worry about "which side of the fence Elizabeth Pixton was on," because she made her feelings clear.

Elizabeth's life was filled with a myriad of pioneer experiences, such as when a whirlwind tore the roof off her house or a snake fell through the dirt roof onto her table set for dinner.

—Elizabeth Cooper Pixton, Brigham Young wagon company (*Tales of Triumph*, vol. 6, 278–280)

Here [in Omaha], we were forced to wait several days for men from Utah who were to take charge of the company. My parents were penniless and were without the necessary cooking utensils to begin the long trip across the plains. One day while we were waiting, some other children and [I] went into some oak brush to play when, right before me, lay a five-dollar gold piece. I picked it up and showed it to the other children. An older girl in the group wanted to give me some bright pieces of cloth for it, but, although I did not know its value, I felt I must take it to father. This I did and he took it to the captain of the company, who told him there would be no chance of finding the owner and for him to use it. Again, in our time of need, we acknowledged the hand of the Lord in helping us.

Again, in our time of need, we acknowledged the hand of the Lord in helping us.

—Marie Abelone Nielsen, emigrated from Denmark aboard the *Kenilworth*, then joined the Andrew H. Scott wagon company in 1866 (Autobiography of Marie Nielsen Robins, familysearch.org; see also see also *Tales of Triumph*, vol. 6, 320–321)

My grandmother heeded the warning voice of the "gospel message" as it reached her home in Glasgow. She evidently had prepared her heart for this wonderful event through study and prayer, and when only a young girl of seventeen, she was baptized a member of The Church of Jesus Christ of Latter-day Saints. She was baptized July 18, 1842. For the next fourteen years [she] remained in Scotland. . . . Her heart grew more restless! She . . . longed for the day when she could lift her voice 'mid the everlasting hills and sing her praises to the all-wise Father who had prepared a place for his faithful saints! Many times in her life, grandmother said to her children, **"I saw the valley before I ever left Scotland."**

—Louise Cowan, speaking of her grandmother Margaret Dalglish Cowan, who emigrated from Scotland before joining the Willie handcart company (Allphin, *Tell My Story, Too*, 25)

From the time we left our home in Denmark, my eleven-year-old brother had been ill. Most of the time so bad he had to be carried from place to place. We left Omaha, August seventh, in Captain Scott's company, and at noon on August 9, just as mother was preparing the meal, my older brother, who was left in the wagon, called, "Oh, Mother! Ditlow is dying!" He had been so anxious to reach Zion where he could rest, but was the first of the company to be left at the side of the trail. In one hour, the train moved on, but before that time a shallow grave had been dug by Father. The little body was wrapped in a blanket and laid away, and the stricken family fell in line with their faces ever to the west.

The morning before his death, one of the teamsters had given him a stick of peppermint candy, which was taken from his hand before death and divided among the children, being the first candy I had ever tasted.

Forty-four others of the company passed away before Salt Lake Valley was reached.

—Marie Abelone Nielsen Robins, emigrated from Denmark aboard the *Kenilworth*, then joined the Andrew H. Scott wagon company (Autobiography of Marie Nielsen Robins, familysearch.org [KWZG-CBF])

Mother's health was poor, and she and my two smaller sisters rode in the wagon most of the way, but I walked the entire distance, being placed in the wagon only when the streams were too deep to be waded.

A company of prospectors was a short distance ahead of us on the plains, and I would often go to their campsites and gather discarded bacon rinds [and] onion and potato peelings and take them to Mother. She would scrape and clean them and make broth that tasted better than the choicest food does now. When we reached Echo Canyon, a terrible storm came up and many of the cattle were frozen to death. The emigrants were so hungry they would have eaten the flesh of the animals, but the officers in charge would not allow [it]. We arrived at the tithing yard in Salt Lake City October 6, 1866, after five months of almost constant traveling.

—Marie Abelone Nielsen Robins, emigrated from Denmark aboard the *Kenilworth* before joining the Scott wagon company (Autobiography of Marie Nielsen Robins, familysearch.org; see also *Tales of Triumph*, 321)

One day we came to a section inhabited by rattlesnakes. Two of us, my friend Mary Hurren and I, would hold hands and jump. It seemed to me we were jumping for more than a mile. Due to the protecting hand of the Lord, we were not harmed. . . .

Ride to Zion © Julie Rogers

When the wagons started out, a number of us children decided to see how long we could keep up with the wagons, in hopes of being asked to ride. At least, that is what my great hope was. One by one they all fell out, until I was the last one remaining, so determined was I that I should get a ride. After what seemed the longest run I ever made before or since, the driver, who was Heber [William Henry] Kimball, called to me, "Say, sissy, would you like a ride?" I answered in my very best manner, "Yes sir." At this he reached over, taking my hand, clucking to his horses to make me run, with legs that seemed to me could run no farther. On we went, to what to me seemed miles. What went through my head at that time was that he was the meanest man that ever lived or that I had ever heard of, and other things that would not be a credit nor would it look well coming from one so young. Just at what seemed the breaking point, he stopped. Taking a blanket, he wrapped me up and lay me in the bottom of the wagon, warm and comfortable. Here I had time to change my mind, as I surely did, knowing full well by doing this he saved me from freezing when taken into the wagon.

—Agnes Caldwell Southworth, emigrated from Scotland aboard the *Thornton* before joining the Willie handcart company (Susan Arrington Madsen, *I Walked to Zion* [Salt Lake City: Desert Book, 1994], 58–59)

At one time Elizabeth [Cunningham Kelly] . . . was left for dead on the plains, as she was thought to be frozen to death. The ground was frozen so hard that they could not dig a grave so they just wrapped her in a blanket and laid the body on the ground and hurried on to make camp for the night, as darkness was fast overtaking them. After they had reached camp, the mother of Elizabeth felt impressed to go back to the child. Her friends ridiculed the idea, but the mother was determined, for she maintained that the child was not dead. She had been promised in Scotland that if she was faithful, that she and all her family would reach Zion in safety. She went back to the child and found her undisturbed by the wolves. She carried the child back to camp and worked over her. Some hot water was spilt on her foot and it caused a quiver to go through the limb. Convinced that she was still alive, they kept up their efforts until they brought her back to life. This is the Elizabeth who lived to be the mother of thirteen children, and the foster mother of three others.

—about Elizabeth Cunningham Kelly, who emigrated from Scotland aboard the *Thornton*, then joined the Willie handcart company ("Olive Binnall was 36 years old when her grandmother, Elizabeth Cunningham Kelly, died, and Olive wrote this history 6 years later. Olive and her grandmother both lived in American Fork, Utah, which adds a further degree of reliability to this account." [Allphin, *Tell My Story, Too*, 22])

The first of the Willie company had been brought into the valley on November 9. Until the last of November others were straggling in, most riding in wagons, a few still grimly hauling their battered carts, still defiantly on their own legs. Margaret Dalglish of the Martin company, a gaunt image of Scottish fortitude, dragged her handful of belongings to the very rim of the valley, but when she looked down and saw the end of it she did something extraordinary. She tugged the cart to the edge of the road and gave it a push and watched it roll and crash and burst apart, scattering into Emigration Canyon the last things she owned on earth. **Then she went on into Salt Lake to start the new life with nothing but her gaunt bones, her empty hands, her stout heart.**

—Wallace Stegner about Margaret Dalglish Cowan (*The Gathering of Zion: The Story of the Mormon Trail* (New York: McGraw Hill, 1964), 255–56)

Mary Ann, with only rags covering her feet, led her snow-blind mother for three days as she pulled the handcart. During this time she carried an ox hoof, and at each camp she would roast it and eat the part that was roasted. This was all she had to eat during those three days.

—Mary Laws, about her mother, Mary Ann Gadd Rowley, and her grandmother Eliza Chapman Gadd, members of the Willie handcart company (Allphin, *Tell My Story, Too*, 31)

During the last few days before relief came, our small allowance of flour was cooked as a gruel and eaten that way. Pieces of rawhide on the handcarts were also cooked to secure what food value there was in them. I remember one morning my father went out and, with a stick, uncovered from the snow a piece of rawhide about a foot square. After washing it in snow water and scraping the hair off, he cut it into small strips and boiled it. Those pieces were then given to us to eat. We were very thankful to receive them and chewed them as we would gum until we secured what nourishment there was in it.

The snow was about eighteen inches deep, and it was bitter cold in the wind. We lacked sufficient clothing and bedding, as we were limited in the amount we could bring. My shoes were worn out, and my feet and legs were badly frozen. I remember being lifted up on the shoulder of one of the men, where I could see a grave which had been dug to bury those that had died during the day. I counted 14 bodies in this one grave. The grave was dug shallow, as no one had strength to dig it very deep, and the soil was frozen and hard. They were buried in the clothes in which they died. Two more members of our company died while these fourteen were being buried. [Rock Creek hollow, October 24]. . . .

When we arrived in Salt Lake City, we camped in the old tithing office lot, which was located where the Hotel Utah now stands. We were met by Uncle George Reeder. When he saw what a pitiful condition we were in, he went for medical aid. Two doctors came back with him. In the meantime, my mother had warmed some water and was engaged in soaking the rags from off my frozen legs and feet. One of the doctors remarked, "She'll never get over this. There's nothing we can do here." He did not expect that I would live more than a day or two at the most. They came back, however, in the morning and informed my father that the only way to save my life would be to have my legs amputated. The doctors informed father that it would be necessary to amputate one leg just above the knee and the other one directly below the knee. My father objected to this and said that his little girl had not walked for a thousand miles across the plains to have her legs cut off. [Mary's mother said to the doctor, "If she dies, she dies with her feet on."] The flesh fell away from the calves of my legs so that it was necessary to grow new flesh. My mother put sweet oil on my legs. I remember that on several occasions after coming to Brigham City that Father walked to Ogden to secure fresh beef to bind on my legs. It was three long years before I was able to walk. . . . ***If I had my life to live over again, I would not want to avoid any of the hardships that I have passed through. I would not want it any different.***

—Mary Hurren Wight, emigrated from England aboard the *Thornton* before joining the Willie handcart company (Mary Hurren Wight, Reminiscences, July 10, 1936, in James G. Willie History, Church History Library, Salt Lake City, https://history.churchofjesuschrist.org/chd/transcript?lang=eng&name=transcript-for-wight-mary-hurren-reminiscences-in-james-g-willie-history)

Having worn out her shoes and going barefoot, Emma was given some hide from . . . dead oxen to wrap around her feet. When that [wore] out, she kept the worn-out pieces and would toast them over the fire to eat. She continued having hard times while she raised her nine children. She crocheted, knitted, and did all kinds of beautiful handwork. She was talented in making beautiful paper flowers, especially roses. She took pride in her appearance and how she dressed. She always wore a bit of white lace at the neck of her dress and made sure her hat was placed just right. Her faith and testimony remained strong to her death.

—Descendants remembering Emma James, who emigrated from England aboard the *Thornton* before joining the Willie handcart company (Allphin, *Tell My Story, Too*, 51)

Toward morning some of the captains who had gone out to gather up the stragglers came into camp bearing the dead body of my father and the badly frozen body of my brother, Reuben. . . . When morning came, Father's body, along with others who had died during the night, were buried in a deep hole. I can see my mother's face as she sat looking at the partly conscious Reuben. Her eyes looked so dead that I was afraid. She didn't sit long, however, for my mother was never one to cry. When it was time to move out, Mother had her family ready to go. She put her invalid son in the cart with the baby, and we joined the train. ***Our mother was a strong woman, and she would see us through anything. . . .***

—Sarah James, emigrated from England aboard the *Thornton* before joining the Willie handcart company (Allphin, *Tell My Story, Too*, 51)

The loaded wagon that came to our camp was from Draper, Utah. George Clawson and Gurnsey Brown were the teamsters. When we got to the foot of the big mountain, the snow was so deep I had to put men's boots on. The teamsters were tall, and so was Esther Brown, and she could step in their tracks, but I could not in hers, and I had to make my own road up both mountains, frequently falling down. The snow was so deep and drifted, but they told us when we got to the top we would see Salt Lake City. We were so thankful and delighted that it seemed to renew our strength and energy. It was the hardest part of my journey, but the thought of being nearly at our journey's end after six months traveling and camping was cheering. When we got to the top of the big mountains, the menfolks took off their hats, and we waved our handkerchiefs.

They then pointed out Salt Lake City, and I could not believe it was, for it looked to me like a patch of sagebrush covered with snow. I could not believe it until we got nearly to it. We arrived in Salt Lake City just at sundown on the thirtieth day of November 1856.

—Elizabeth White, emigrated from England aboard the *Horizon* before joining the Hunt wagon company (Allphin, *Tell My Story, Too*, 369; see also Daughters of Utah Pioneer history files)

One day in mid-ocean, the ship sprang a leak. The anchor was lowered while the pumps were set to work. I heard a sailor report that the trunk room was being flooded. Happy childhood! Little sensed I of the real danger that threatened us. It was barely noon. I went by myself, knelt down with full childish faith, and prayed: "Our Father

in Heaven, please don't let my new dress get wet." And I finished up with, "Now I lay me down to sleep, I pray the Lord my soul to keep; if I should die before I wake, I pray the Lord my soul to take. Amen." I think the listening angels must have smiled at that prayer; but in spite of the fact that my dress was in the very bottom of the trunk, it was not damaged in the least. We found so many interesting things to do that the voyage of six weeks did not seem nearly so irksome to us as it did to some of the older ones; but when someone shouted, "Land, I see land!" I believe Columbus himself could not have been much happier than we were."

—Amelia Eliza Slade Bennion, emigrated from England aboard the *William Tapscott*, then joined the Warren Snow wagon company in 1864 (*Our Pioneer Heritage*, vol. 2, 217, https://www.familysearch.org/photos/artifacts/84104380)

[Sarah was] heard saying that **she would rather die than give up her testimony of the truthfulness of the restored Gospel of Jesus Christ.**

—Descendants remembering Sarah James, who emigrated from England aboard the *Thornton* before joining the Willie handcart company (Allphin, *Tell My Story, Too*, 51; Andrew D. Olsen, *The Price We Paid*, [Salt Lake City: Deseret Book], 2006)

We continued on our journey with many hardships until we reached [Fort] Laramie, Wyoming, about October 8, 1856. We rested here for a short time, and it was necessary for us to dispose of our prized possessions and buy cornmeal, beans, and other food stuffs, as our supply was gone. We were rationed to a pound of flour per day. The portion was decreased several times until all of our flour was gone. The captain was very kind to mother and gave her some of the flour sacks to scrape off with a knife what little flour was left along with the lint. With this she was able to make some cakes and mush to help sustain life. . . . On our way, we camped at a gulch called "Martin's Ravine." Here we suffered terribly with the cold. It was only with the power of God that we survived. When we reached Devil's Gate, we met wagons from Salt Lake City with provisions and clothing waiting for us. From this time on, the journey was better and much easier.

—Josephine Hartley, emigrated from England aboard the *Horizon* before joining the Martin handcart company (Allphin, *Tell My Story, Too*, 218; see also familysearch.org)

Eddie died as we were nearing Green River. This final stroke proved too much for Mother, and she became very, very ill. One day as Rhoda and I came near the wagon, we heard voices. "Yes, Sister Slade, your children will be cared for." The wild fears that arose in my breast seemed to smother me. Baby Charles and Eddie, and now Mother! Taking my sister by the hand, we ran off some distance into the sagebrush and, kneeling down, we prayed in all our childish anguish, "Please, Heavenly Father, don't let Mother die. Please make her better, in the name of Jesus, Amen." We felt sure then she would get well. Next morning she was much better, and after some days she was trying again to take her share of the burdens. . . .

The last day of our journey our food gave out and we became really hungry. Towards evening we entered Emigration Canyon. As we came into the valley, we could see in the distance the glow of a big bonfire that had been [lit] to welcome us. About ten o'clock we stopped at the square where the City and County building now stands.

Such laughing and crying, such hugs and kisses! Soon we were seated around the big fire, while willing hands, backed by warm hearts, served us with everything that the little settlement could afford in the way of delicious hot food. There were mashed potatoes and gravy, chicken and vegetables, pie and cake. Then, when we just couldn't cram another delicious morsel, I noticed by the light of the fire, a tempting green slope. "Come on," I said to the girls, "let's roll down here," and roll we did, to our hearts' content, entirely unreproved by the older folk. They were "home" at last and too happy to notice it.

—Amelia Eliza Slade Bennion, emigrated from England aboard the *William Tapscott*, then joined the Warren Snow wagon company in 1864 (*Our Pioneer Heritage*, vol. 2, 227)

Father and my oldest brother stopped to help bury a member of our company. Mother waited with them as she was helping to draw the cart with the heaviest load. We children went on with our load until we came to a river [that] we could not ford. It was snowing and blowing. Father's strength gave out. He made every possible effort to continue, but without success. Mother was placed in an awful position. Her husband unable to go farther, and her little children far ahead, starving and freezing, what could she do? Father said, "Go to the children; we will get in if we can." She hurried on with a prayer in her heart for Father's deliverance and our safety. She found us by the river, and with her aid, we waded through. Our [wet] clothing . . . was soon covered with ice, and our shoes frozen on our feet. Camp was reached but we had no one to fix our tent, as Father and Brother were behind. We watched and listened for their coming, hoping and praying for the best. At last they were brought in, but death had claimed our father.

—Mary Ann James, emigrated from England aboard the *Thornton* before joining the Willie handcart company
(Allphin, *Tell My Story, Too*, 51)

Mother, in company with a young lady, Christena McNeil, who was making the trip under Mother's care, visited one of the generals in command at the fort to obtain

Christena © Julie Rogers

permission to trade some trinkets and silver spoons for flour and meat. The officer said he himself could not use any of the things but to leave the young lady in his office while mother went to another station, where he assured her she would be able to obtain the things she desired. . . . During her absence, the officer used the time in trying to persuade Christena to stay there, proposing to her and showing her the gold he had, telling her what a fine lady he would make of her. Then he tried discouraging her, pointing out to her how the handcart company would never reach Utah because of the severe cold, and that they would die of cold and hunger and exposure. Like all noble girls, and true to the cause for which she had left her native Scotland, she told him in plain language she would take her chances with the others even though it might mean death. She was greatly relieved to have Mother return. The officer, however, seemed to admire her very much for her loyalty to her faith and gave her a large cured ham and wished her well in her chosen adventure.

—Agnes Caldwell, about her mother's friend, Christina McNeil, who emigrated from Scotland before joining the Willie handcart company (Allphin, *Tell My Story Too*, 73)

We prepared to leave our happy little home for the land of Zion. I remember how rough the North Sea was. . . . How well I remember the day we went on board the ship at Liverpool. It was the second day of May and my eleventh birthday, and on the fourth we set sail. Our trip across the ocean was seven weeks and four days, and we arrived in New York. After a few days, we left for Iowa City. My father had intended to purchase a team of horses and wagon to bring his family, but on account of so many poor Saints, they were promised by those in authority if they would come with the handcart company and help others to come that not one of the family should be

Day After Day © Julie Rogers

lost, which blessing was fulfilled, though we suffered much on the way. . . . Cold and storm came early that year, and as we neared the mountains, suffering became intense, especially from hunger and cold. I think every one had their darkest hour then; our family certainly did. One day the boys pulled the cart out of the line and lay down beside it saying, "Mother, we can't go another step." We children stood by crying, thinking of the terrors in store for us. . . . The train had gone on way ahead of us, but oh! How thankful we were to reach camp after dark. . . .

My brothers helped shovel the snow and picked the frozen ground to bury in one grave fourteen bodies, and the last one of mother's handwoven linen sheets was covered

over them before the dirt was put in. The thing I regret most in all that terrible time was taking a piece of bread from a dead woman's pocket. She was a woman I had walked with day after day, and I knew she had this bread she had not eaten. How well I remember now the fourteen that were buried in one grave. My two brothers just older than myself helped to prepare the grave, and my mother [helped] to wrap the bodies as best they could. [We stayed there] two nights and one day. . . . We were helped the last miles of the journey into Salt Lake, but after what a lot of suffering. I wish we might have been allowed to forget it.

—Mette Kirstine Mortensen, emigrated from Denmark aboard the *Thornton* before joining the Willie handcart company (Allphin, *Tell My Story, Too*, 81)

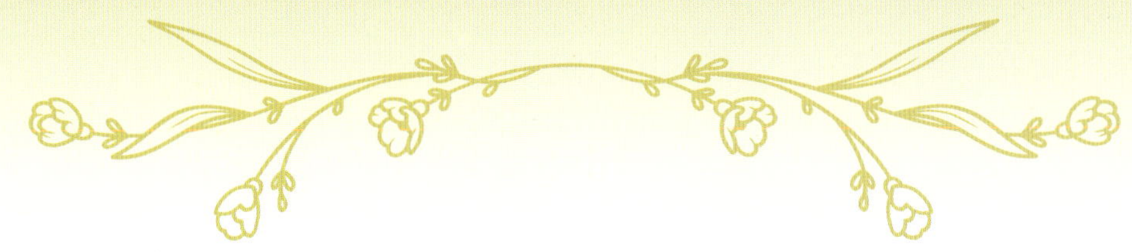

We walked by the river day after day, following the Platte six hundred miles, crossing and recrossing it about ninety times. We had to have stout hearts and great faith in meeting these great trials, misfortunes and sickness, pain and death, burying our beloved dead ones who gave their lives for the sake of the gospel. We wept as we went on our journey. We went before the Lord and pleaded for Him to make good the promises [that] were given us by His servant when we were in old Denmark. How we implored Him to raise the sick and give us strength to carry our burdens without complaining, for we had the lame to haul on our handcarts, the maimed to care for, and our beloved dead ones to bury by the wayside, never to see again the place where they were laid to rest.

[We] were often reminded of Jeremiah's vision and prophecy [of the last days] recorded in the 31st chapter [v.6–9, 12–13]: 'For there shall be a day, that the watchmen upon . . . Ephraim shall cry, Arise ye, and let us go up to Zion unto the Lord our God.

For thus saith the Lord; Sing with gladness for Jacob, and shout among the chief of the nations: publish ye, praise ye, and say, O Lord, save thy people, the remnant of Israel. Behold, I will bring them from the north country, and gather them from the coasts of the earth, and with them the blind and the lame, the woman with child and her that travaileth with child together: a great company shall return thither. They shall come with weeping, and with supplications will I lead them: I will cause them to walk by the rivers of waters in a straight way, wherein they shall not stumble: for I am a father to Israel, and Ephraim is my firstborn. . . . Therefore they shall come and sing in the height of Zion, and shall flow together to the goodness of the Lord. . . . Then shall [they] rejoice in the dance, both young . . . and old together: for I will turn their mourning into joy, and will comfort them, and make them rejoice from their sorrow."

I will turn their mourning into joy, and will comfort them, and make them rejoice from their sorrow."

—Helena Mortensen, emigrated from Denmark aboard the *Thornton*, then joined the Willie handcart company (Allphin, *Tell My Story, Too*, 82–83; see also Daughters of Utah Pioneers history files, Parowan Daughters of Utah Pioneers Museum)

I can't remember when I first knew my Aunt Jane Bell, or when I first heard the story of Grandmother Cranney and her trek across the plains. As a child I remember being aware that Grandmother had been with the [Willie] handcart company and that she had suffered a great deal on the way to Salt Lake City.

I remember hearing about Aunt Jane being so sick [lying in the handcart] and how Grandmother didn't dare stop to take care of her and she would just go on and call to her small son, Chris, and ask him if Jane was dead yet. I used to think about this and wonder how she could have stood it.

When I was about fifteen, Aunt Jane came up to the ranch in Star Valley to visit us. She was such a little, quick, spunky character that I loved her very dearly. . . . While she was visiting us she told me the story of her mother's experience on the plains. . . . Grandmother Cranney and the other members of the [Willie] handcart company were in terrible shape. The supplies had dwindled until nearly all of the people were starving. Grandmother was out gathering some buffalo chips to make a small fire to warm what little food that they had left for her children. She had on a long, full apron and had almost filled it with the buffalo chips. A man came up to her and talked to her and asked how the members of the company were. She told him that most of them were starving, and he asked her to follow him and maybe he could help a little. Aunt Jane said that her mother shook out her apron and went with him. They went over a small hill and were out of sight of the camp. In the side of the hill was sort of a cave, and he led Grandmother into the cave. On one side of the cave was a lot of dried buffalo meat hanging up.

The man loaded as much meat in Grandmother's apron as she could carry and told her to share with the other people. Then he led her out of the cave and to the top of a small hill and pointed out the camp below and told her not to get lost. As Grandmother turned back to him to thank him, after she had looked where he had pointed to the camp, he had disappeared. She looked for the cave and could find no trace of it, but she still had the dried meat. She went back to camp and divided the meat out to the ones that were in the most need and it saved many lives.

Onward with Faith © Sandra Rast

Years later when Aunt Jane was an elderly woman, she was in Pocatello, Idaho, visiting her daughter. It was on Mother's Day, and her daughter took her to church with her. I remember Aunt Jane said that she hesitated about going because she didn't want to take some other mother's gift, since she didn't belong to that ward. During this same program, an elderly man got up to talk, and he told of coming to Utah with his family when he was a small boy with the [Willie] handcart company, and how they were starving and some sister in the company had received some dried meat in some miraculous way and had shared it, and he was very grateful to that sweet sister.

Aunt Jane said she cried when she heard this because so many people had made fun of her story of her mother's experience until she had almost come to doubt it herself. She talked to the gentleman and told him that she was a baby with that company and that it was her mother who had received the meat. She said that it was wonderful to have another witness of this wonderful experience.

—June Cranney Monson, granddaughter of Elizabeth Crook Panting, who emigrated from England aboard the *Thornton* before joining the Willie handcart company (Allphin, *Tell My Story, Too*, 102; see also T.C. Christensen and Jolene Allphin, *More Than Miracles*, 30–33 and T.C. Christensen, *Second Witness: The Elizabeth Panting Story*, DVD, 2014)

I was left a widow with seven children under twelve years of age and the stepchildren of William's first marriage. I was very grateful for the gospel of Jesus Christ and the comfort it gave me. I knew that our parting was only temporary, and that viewed from the eternities, this was but a fleeting moment. I also knew that no matter how fleeting a moment it was, I had to make the best of it. I had a very real job to do. The children had to be fed and clothed, but the big task and the one I must accomplish [was] to get us all to Zion. I must be among the people of my faith, and I must get the temple work done for us. Each person that could earn money at all was required to work. . . . Samuel was only seven and John nine, but they worked in a brick yard tramping mud to be used for bricks. I would help the little fellows across a narrow, dangerous bridge to go to work at daylight, and at night I would meet them and help them home. The girls, even eleven-year-old Elizabeth, worked late in the night making kid gloves, doing mock frocking and other needlework. We did this in our home. Then at the end of the week, I would take [the gloves] to market, where they were sold to the gentry. Our savings were meager,

[but] with the perpetual aid fund, we were able to book passage. . . . Only one of my stepchildren sailed with us, Eliza, a sweet girl, with very frail health. . . .

We were delayed in Iowa City. Handcarts had to be made, supplies gathered, oxen caught and broken to pull the heavy supply wagons, everything that even hinted of being a luxury, must be eliminated. There were many keepsakes that I wanted to take but couldn't. But there was one thing I didn't consider a luxury and that was my feather-bed. . . . No matter how I folded it, it was too bulky. . . . But a feather-bed is a feather-bed, and when it came to choosing between Zion and a feather-bed, well, it was a little too late to turn my back on Zion, so I ripped it open and emptied the feathers on the ground and used the tick to cover the supplies on the handcart. . . .

There came a time when there seemed to be no food at all. Some of the men left to hunt buffalo. Night was coming and there was no food for the evening meal. I asked God's help as I always did. I got on my knees, remembering two hard sea biscuits that were still in my trunk. They were not large, and were so hard they couldn't be broken. Surely, that was not enough to feed 8 people, but 5 loaves and 2 fishes were not enough to feed 5,000 people either, but through a miracle, Jesus had done it. So, with God's help, nothing is impossible. I found the biscuits and put them in a dutch oven and covered them with water and asked for God's blessing, then I put the lid on the pan and set it on the coals. ***When I took off the lid a little later, I found the pan filled with food. I kneeled with my family and thanked God for his goodness.***

—Ann Jewell Rowley, emigrated from England aboard the *Thornton* before joining the Willie handcart company (Allphin, *Tell My Story, Too*, 116)

I will not dwell upon the hardships we endured, nor the hunger and cold, but I like to tell of the goodness of God unto us. One day, especially, stands out from among the remainder. The wind blew fresh, as if its breezes came from the sea. It kept blowing harder until it became fierce. Clouds arose; the thunder and lightning were appalling. Even the ox teams ahead refused to face the storm. Our captain, who always rode a mule, dismounted and stepped into the middle of the road, bared his head to the storm, and every man, as he came up, stood by him with bared head—one hundred carts, their pullers and pushers, looking to their captain for counsel. The captain said, "Let us pray." And there was offered such a prayer! He told the Lord our circumstances. He talked to God, as one man talks to another, and as if the Lord was very near. I felt that He was, and many others felt the same. Then the storm parted to the right and to the left! We hurried on to camp, got our tents pitched, and some fires built, when the storm burst in all its fury! We had camped on a side hill, and the water ran through the tents in little creeks.

—Elizabeth "Betsey" Smith, emigrated from Scotland aboard the *Thornton* before joining the Willie handcart company (Betsy Smith Goodwin, "The Tired Mother," *Improvement Era*, July 1919, 778; see also Robert's story in rescuer section and Euphemia Mitchell's story in Willie section, *Tell My Story, Too*, 75–76, 410)

LET US PRAY

Let Us Pray © Julie Rogers

My parents, relatives, and friends did all in their power to keep me from coming to America, but I had the spirit of gathering, and the Lord opened up my way, and I came to Utah in 1856 with the handcart company. Brother Willie was our captain, Millen Atwood was his councilor. . . . We waded through the cold streams many times, but we murmured not, for our faith in God and our testimony of His work were supreme. Only once did my courage fail. One cold, dreary afternoon, my feet having been frosted, I felt that I could go no further, and withdrew a little from the company, and sat down to await the end, being somewhat in a stupor. After a time, I was aroused by a voice, which seemed as audible as anything could be, which spoke to my very soul

of the promises and blessings I had received, and which should surely be fulfilled, and that I had a mission to perform in Zion. I received strength, and was filled with the Spirit of the Lord, and arose and traveled on with a light heart. As I reached camp, I found a search party ready to go back to find me, dead or alive. . . .

I am thankful that I was counted worthy to be a pioneer and a handcart girl. It prepared me to endure hard times in my future life. I often think of the songs we sang to encourage us on our toilsome journey. ***It was hard to endure, but the Lord gave us strength and courage.***

—Susannah Stone, emigrated from England aboard the *Thornton* before joining the Willie handcart company (Allphin, *Tell My Story, Too*, 132)

"For the Lord's sake bring my girl on the ship and don't leave her behind." There was just the one plank to walk on from the dock to the ship, and Father and Mother were so afraid I would fall off into the water. The sailors said, "Miss, do you think you can walk this plank?" I told them I thought I could, but they thought I might get dizzy and fall off into the water, so they were very kind. One man went on the plank before me and took my right hand; the second man came behind me on the plank and took my left hand. They said if I slipped they would save me from going in the water. . . . There was great anxiety with them all when they saw me walking on just one plank with two sailors holding my hand, and there was great rejoicing when I was safe on the vessel with them all.

—Patience Loader, emigrated from England aboard the *John J. Boyd* before joining the Martin handcart company (Patience Loader Rozsa Archer, *Recollections of Past Days: The Autobiography of Patience Loader Rozsa Archer*, ed. Sandra Ailey Petree [Logan, UT: Utah State University Press, 2006] 49, https://digitalcommons.usu.edu/cgi/viewcontent.cgi?article=1036&context=usupress_pubs)

We did not get but very little meat, as the bone had been picked the night before, and we did not have only the half of a small biscuit, as we only [were] having four ounces of flour a day. This we divided into portions so we could have a small piece three times a day. This we ate with thankful hearts, and we always asked God to bless to our use and that it would strengthen our bodies day by day so that we could perform our duties. And I can testify that our Heavenly Father heard and answered our prayers and we [were] blessed with health and strength day by day to endure the severe trials we had to pass through on that terrible journey before we got to Salt Lake City. We know that if God had not been with us that our strength would have failed us. . . . I can say we put our trust in God and He heard and answered our prayers and brought us through to the valleys.

—Patience Loader, emigrated from England aboard the *John J. Boyd* before joining the Martin handcart company (Patience Loader Rozsa Archer, *Recollections of Past Days: The Autobiography of Patience Loader Rozsa Archer*, ed. Sandra Ailey Petree [Logan, UT: Utah State University Press, 2006], 86)

One day when the company had stopped for dinner, she and another lady companion strolled out a little way from camp, [were] so very tired, and foot sore, and weary, they lay down thinking to have a little rest, and fell off to sleep. When the company was ready for going on, they couldn't be found . . . couldn't be [woken] by their shouts. The company went on while they slept behind a large brush. When they awoke, and finding themselves left and alone, they were very frightened and horrified at seeing that night was coming on and they were alone in the wilderness. What should they do? They screamed . . . [and] decided to follow the tracks. . . . [They] ran and they hollered, but to no avail; when dark came on, they had not found their company. . . . They prayed and they traveled. . . . Wolves and coyotes barking and howling all around them frightened them terribly, but they kept on going, silently praying . . . finally coming to a stream of water. Feeling sure that [their] company had crossed this stream, they stood on the bank and shouted several times, and [finally] heard voices on the

Angels Will Attend Thee © Sandra Rast

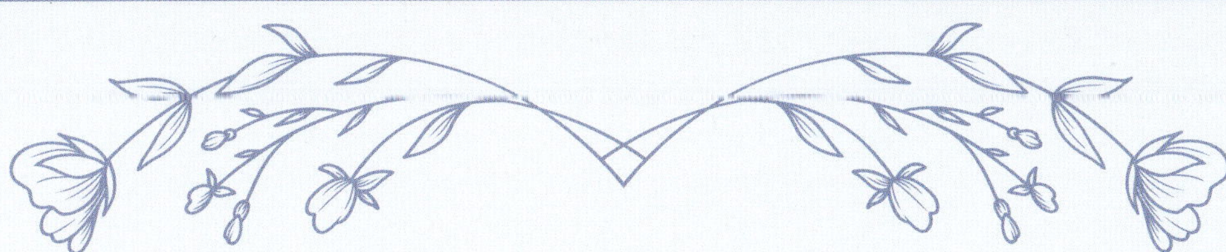

other side. It was two men . . . that had heard them hollering, and [were] coming to rescue them. Again they offered up a prayer of thanks and gratitude to God for his kindness and holy hand in guiding them to their company. Soon they were safely in camp.

—Elizabeth Xavier Tait, who emigrated from India before joining the Willie handcart company (Allphin, *Tell My Story, Too*, 136)

One day while on the ship, I was up in the cooking room cooking dinner. It was so crowded, there was hardly standing room. The people were all cooking their dinner. One man was boiling soup in a milk can. When he took the soup from the stove, he lifted it over my head in order to carry it through the crowd. While doing so, somebody knocked him, and it fell out of his hand on my back. My father stood outside waiting for me to come with the dinner. I ran out to him, and he said, "Come downstairs and let's get some oil." So we ran down the steps and got one of the elders to administer to me. It was better in a few minutes; the pain had entirely gone, and I never felt any more of it. Some of the soup went on the hands of the man who had spilled it on me. He ran and put his hands in a bucket of cold water and wasn't administered to. He, not being a convert, wouldn't hear [of] having the elders pray for him. His hands were blistered and they didn't get better until two weeks. . . .

We had been five weeks on the sea when we landed in Boston. We were very glad to walk on land again. . . . Then we started on a journey . . . across the plains. . . .

After pitching our tents [near Devil's Gate], we lay down on the ground to get some sleep and rest. In the night the tents all blew over. It was all ice and snow where I was [lying], and when the tents blew off I didn't wake up, I was so tired. One man came and looked at me. He called some more men over, saying, "I wonder if she is dead." He patted me on the head, and just then I opened my eyes. He jumped back. I tried to raise my head but found that my hair was frozen to the ground. They chopped the ice all around my hair, and I got up and went over to the fire and melted the large pieces of ice that were clinging to my hair. The men laughed to think that I could lie there all night with my hair frozen in the ice but were very glad that I wasn't dead. This same night the handcarts all blew away, and some of us had to walk until we met some other wagons. Mrs. Unthanks got her feet frozen and had to have them taken off, but when we met more wagons, we could all ride. There were four men in our tent, and all of them died, father dying first.

—Mary Barton, emigrated from England aboard the *Horizon* before joining the Martin handcart company (Allphin, *Tell My Story, Too*, 166–167)

At last we found ourselves encamped in a ravine near Devil's Gate with just four ounces of flour to each person per day for four days. A great number of people died, sometimes half a dozen a day, and on one occasion sixteen persons were buried in one day in one grave. People would walk until exhausted and then drop down by the wayside dead, leaving

The Blue Angel © Julie Rogers

their bodies to be eaten by wolves, as the survivors, on account of the frozen ground, were not able to dig graves deep enough to secure them. . . . We climbed mountains to get icicles off sage brush and melted the snow to obtain water where with to mix our flour. At Devil's Gate [Red Buttes] the people were called together for prayer and asked if they were willing to die if the Lord so willed it, or if they were sorry they had come. They all answered that they were willing to die if the Lord so willed it, but they were not sorry they had come. Almost at the same moment was witnessed the approach of Joseph A. Young on a white horse. He was hailed by us as the arrival of an angel.

—Alice Brooks, emigrated from England aboard the *Horizon* before joining the Martin handcart company (Allphin, *Tell My Story, Too*, 184)

That night [of Alpha Jacque's birth], my sister Zilpah Jacques was confined at twelve o'clock, and my sister Tamar was very sick with mountain fever. My sister got [through her labor and delivery] quite well. . . . The next morning we got ready to start. The captain came to our tent and told us to be ready to start as soon as we could get ready. There lay my sister Zilpah on the ground . . . She was lying on some quilts in one corner of the tent, and my sister Tamar was lying on quilts in the other corner of the tent, neither of the poor things able to move. The captain, Edward Martin, said, "Put them up in the wagon," as there was a wagon for the sick who were unable to walk. I asked, "Can one of us ride with them to take care of them?" He said, "No, they will have to take care of themselves." Then I said, "They will not go. We will stay here for a day or two and take care of our two sick sisters."

So we were left there all alone as the company started about seven o'clock that morning. . . . When night came, my poor father and my brother-in-law, John Jacques, had to be up all night to make a big fire to keep the wolves away from us. I never heard such a terrible howling of wolves in my life as we experienced that lonesome night. We were all very glad to see daylight . . . Brother Joseph A. Young [came] on horseback riding at great speed to our camp to see what was the cause of the big fire. They had watched the light all night. . . . When he came into the tent and saw my sister with her newborn babe lying on the ground on some quilts, he was overcome with sympathy. The tears ran down his cheeks. Then he blessed my sister and tried to comfort and cheer her by saying, "Well, Sister Jacques, I suppose you will name your boy 'Handcart,' having been born under such circumstances?" "No," she said, "I will want a prettier name than that for him." . . .

[We] made ready to start on our journey again. We packed our handcart, struck our tent, packed it on my handcart, then lay my sister Tamar on that. Then Brother Jacques packed his cart, then put his wife, my sister, and her two children on the cart. We tied the tent poles alongside of the cart. Our cooking utensils we tied under the

Rescue Me, Robert Taylor Burton © Julie Rogers

cart. . . . This was very [hard] on my poor, dear, sick father after having to be up all night, no rest or sleep. . . . It surely did prove that God was with us, for my poor father [James Loader] seemed better that day than he had been for a week past. ***Surely God gave him new strength that day, for we traveled twenty-two miles before we came up with the company. . . .***

[While traveling to catch up to the handcart company], we were overtaken by Brother William Cluff [who had ridden out from Florence] after Brother Joseph A. Young got back there to camp and told the brethren who it was that kept the fire. . . . He fetched a rope with him and tied it to our handcart and then to the pommel of his saddle and gave us a rest. . . . I was very thankful, more on account of our poor, sick father than for us girls because we were young and healthy in those days.

—Patience Loader, emigrated from England aboard the *John J. Boyd* before joining the Martin handcart company (Patience Loader Rozsa Archer, *Recollections of Past Days: The Autobiography of Patience Loader Rozsa Archer*, ed. Sandra Ailey Petree [Logan, UT: Utah State University Press, 2006] 63–66; see also *Tell My Story, Too*, 253–54)

After we had got all our baggage on board the ship, we found the ship would not sail until the next day, so I said to my father and mother that I would go back and stay all night with my sister, as we left my sister Tamar to stay with my sister Zilpah to help her get ready to leave in July. In the afternoon I left them to go down to the ship again, and when I got there, lo and behold, to my great surprise, the ship was in readiness to start out. The men were just taking away the last plank. There were all my folks standing on deck, watching anxiously for me and shouting [at] the top of their voices,

My mother was healed by the power of God. She had faith in the ordinance of prayers and anointing by the elders. My mother lived twenty-three years after coming to Utah and died a faithful Latter-Day Saint. . . . I am here to praise His holy name. . . . I could say much of our suffering, of those who are dead as well as the living, all martyrs to the truth, of which

I am one. I have suffered much and could tell a sad tale but do not wish to complain. The Lord is with me and will help me through. I live to praise His holy name and thank Him for His blessings to me. I pray I may be faithful to the end of my days.

—Elizabeth Wright, emigrated from England aboard the *Horizon* before joining the Martin handcart company (Allphin, *Tell My Story, Too,* 334)

When they crossed the Platte [River] for the first time, Emily had gone . . . with some other children to gather flowers. When they started to cross the river, Marion thought Emily had been carried across with the rest of the children. When everyone was over, she looked for Emily and saw to her dismay that the child had been left and was running, her arms laden with flowers, toward the fording place. The child thought others had waded and seemed intent on wading alone.

Marion called frantically to the child, "Go back, go back," gesturing wildly to her.

It seemed no one sensed her danger immediately and no one offered to go after the child. Marion cried out, "Isn't there someone who could go after my child?" It was necessary for one of the brethren to swim across and bring the child over. His name we would like to know.

After they passed Ft. Laramie, it was deemed advisable to curtail the [daily] allowance [of flour] to three-quarter pound to make the food hold out as long as possible. Later it fell to one-half pound and subsequently still lower. They were advised by the leaders to divide the allowance of food into three portions, one for breakfast, one for dinner and one for the evening meal. Some were obedient and some hungrily ate all at the first or second meal. These suffered most through their lack of wisdom. Grandmother [Marion] made two sacks in which to store the dinner and evening meals' worth of flour. She then hid it in the sleeves of her dress to keep it for later use. The flour cakes were made of flour and water only. They didn't have salt. Emily got sick without salt and asked for it. . . . This was a great trial for a girl of [nine] because she could remember the comforts of home in Dublin.

Grandmother told that the obedient ones suffered the least. Some, tired at night, exhausted and weak, would lie down to sleep in their wet shoes. The advice had been given to remove them and dry the feet at night. Some of them had their feet frozen and suffered in later years as a result. Nothing short of a miracle enabled her to cross the plains in the dead of winter, a widow with a little girl to care for. They arrived in Salt Lake City on November 30, 1856. She was taken to the home of Margaret Judd Clauson, wife of Hiram Clauson, who was bishop of the Eighteenth Ward. Margaret Clauson and my grandmother became lifelong friends.

—Marion (Fleming) Marshall, emigrated from England on the *Horizon* before joining the Martin handcart company (Allphin, *Tell My Story, Too*, 256)

As I was going back to where Mother was sitting, I found a pie in the road. I picked it up and gave it to mother to eat, and after resting awhile we started on our journey, thanking God for His blessings. A few miles before we reached camp, we met my father coming out to meet us. What a joyful meeting that was. We arrived in camp at 10:00 p.m. Many times . . . ***Mother felt like giving up and quitting; but then she would remember how wonderful the Lord had been to spare her so many times, and she offered a prayer of gratitude instead. . . .***

On entering the water, our first impulse was to turn back and not wade across. The water was so cold that it sent pains right to the bone and the muscles cramped. We steadied ourselves as we held onto the cart and pushed. Father pulled. By the time

we got across, our limbs were so numb that we could hardly keep from falling as we trudged along. The north wind cut like a sharp knife. We finally camped where we could get some cottonwood and willows for firewood. . . . We were so fatigued and hungry that we would sometimes stop and get rawhide to chew on, as our food was diminished. We tried to keep a little flour as long as we could to make porridge for the children; at first it was biscuits; then pancakes; then porridge. Often we would cook a hide, or a piece of it, to get a little strength. It being winter, we could not find weeds to help out.

—Louisa Mellor, emigrated from England aboard the *Horizon* before joining the Martin handcart company (Allphin, *Tell My Story, Too*, 271; see also *Life history and writings of John Jaques*, including Stella Jacques Bell diary of the Martin handcart company, 1978)

We arrived at Devil's Gate about the 1st of November. On account of the nightly fatalities of the male members of our company for two or three weeks previously, there were many widows in our camp, and the women and children had to pitch and put up the tents, shoveling the snow away with tin plates, etc., making our beds on the ground and getting up in the morning with melted snow and lye on our clothing. This hard service continued with all that were able to endure it till we nearly reached the south pass, and one night I dropped to the ground in a dead faint with my baby in my arms. I had some pepper pods with me. In recovering from my stupor, I took some of them to warm and to recover my strength. During these times we had only a little thin flour gruel two or three times a day, and this was meager nourishment for a mother with a nursing baby.

My husband died and was buried near Devil's Gate, and the ground was frozen so hard that the men had a difficult task in digging the grave deep enough in which to inter him and nine others that morning, and it is more than probable that several were only covered with snow. [This was likely in Martin's Cove.] Here I was left a widow with two young children. The boy [John] became so weak that he could not stand alone, and I had to sit and hold both of them in the relief wagons. At times most of us had to walk after being met by the teams from Salt Lake, and late in the day and towards the evening my shoes would nearly freeze to my feet, and at one time in taking [them] off, some of the skin and flesh came off with them. Some of the bones of my feet were left bare and my hands were severely frozen. . . .

After arriving in Salt Lake November 30, 1856, with two children . . . the clothes I stood up in were all of my earthly possessions in a strange land, without kin or relatives. . . . I have always been proud to know that I had the individual courage to accept and embrace the faith and join the Church, to which I have ever been steadfast from that day to this. Though the sufferings were terrible I passed [through] in the handcart journey across the plains, I am still thankful that the Lord preserved my life and made it possible for me to reach Zion. . . . ***After all that I have endured and passed through . . . my testimony is that the gospel of Jesus Christ of Latter-day Saints is true.***

—Alice Fish Walsh (Strong), emigrated from England aboard the *Horizon* before joining the Martin handcart company (Allphin, *Tell My Story, Too*, 319; see also Adam D. Olsen, "Gather to Zion: 'This I have done for Him,'" *Church News*, December 30, 2006)

On the 28th [19th] of October, Sunday afternoon, we crossed the Platte River for the last time. That evening the snow fell about eighteen inches deep. . . . The camp moved about nine miles to a bluff, called by us, the Red Point. We were there nine days; the snow was then about two feet deep. We had only one-fourth of a pound of flour per day to eat. My husband was taken sick. I called in the elders to administer to him, and he was healed immediately. I went to bed and a heavenly messenger came to my bedside

Sunday Morn © Sandra Rast

and said, "Cheer up, Sister Wignall, there are mule teams, horse teams, and ox teams coming to meet you with provisions and clothing from the valley, and tomorrow morning when Mary Ann (Riley) is combing your hair, there will be a man with two pack mules come into camp." Sure enough, just as she was combing my hair about 9 a.m. (there was a great shout). Joseph A. Young and a man who now lives in Provo, I have forgotten his name, rode into camp just as I had been told.

—Grace Slater Wignall, emigrated from England aboard the *Horizon* before later joining the Martin handcart company (Allphin, *Tell My Story, Too*, 331)

We listened to the missionaries of a new church. "Mormons," they were called. We knew it was true and were baptized. My father became an elder and home missionary in Devonshire. Most of our friends and loved ones turned against us because of our beliefs. My father longed to go to America to be with the Saints and to be taught firsthand from a prophet of God. Father propositioned the pension board for a specified sum in lieu of monthly payments. That way he could buy passage for our family and we could join the Saints in Zion. It was so hard to say goodbye to close friends and sell possessions for whatever we could get, even giving them away. But we had to have enough for passage and for so many things in America if we were going to make it. My parents, my older brother, Robert [21], my younger brother, Fredrick [14], and I, being in my nineteenth year, set off sail to America on the vessel *S. Curling*. On board, I met a wonderful man by the name of John DeGroot Oakley, who was returning to his family after a four-year mission to England and France. Since he had lived among the Saints and knew Joseph Smith personally, I had many questions to ask him, which passed the time and made the several-week voyage seem much shorter. Also, before coming into the Boston harbor, I became very ill with chicken pox. I draped a heavy veil over my hat and face to hide them when we left the ship on the 23rd of May 1856. America! We made it. The land of promises, hopes, freedom, and dreams. . . . The sound of [America] was wonderfully exciting.

We started out with much hope and promise for a new life in Utah and plenty of provisions, we thought. However, before we reached Devil's Gate, the provisions were very low. . . . Father called our family to his wagon and said, **"I have pointed you Zionward, and I want you never to turn back."** . . . [After he died] we rolled him in half our wagon cover and buried him in a shallow grave. The ground was frozen, and we simply had no means or time to do more. Seven others died that night and were buried there. That same night there was a terrible storm that dropped almost a foot of new snow. The next morning I managed to yoke up the oxen, but my grief was so strong I flung myself over Father's grave and sobbed until others pulled me away. Winter was settling in and there was precious little time left to get to Utah before we became permanently snowbound. I put on my father's boots, slicker, and hat, and drove the slow, plodding team of oxen in danger of freezing and starving. You simply cannot imagine how bad it was. I shared what rations we had with the starving children who had lost their mothers and whose feet were frozen and toes gone.

I remember well the bright moonlight night about 11 o'clock, when fresh provisions and teams arrived. Even our sea biscuits were nearly gone . . . [we having] been on scant rations for weeks. How our hearts swelled inside with thankfulness as these great rescuers, who put their own lives at risk, began cooking hot bread over the fires.

—Louisa Jones, emigrated from England aboard the *S. Curling* before joining the Hodgetts wagon company (Allphin, *Tell My Story, Too*, 346–347; see also familysearch.org)

The campfires at night were very good times. We sang the Church hymns, and they inspired us. "Come, Come Ye Saints" [was] my favorite, and we were happy in our labors. A bond of love and friendship was amongst us. We learned the value of resting and keeping the Sabbath day. We did not choose to remember the pains of hunger and the cold but wanted to remember the goodness of God unto us, as dear Mother Bain Smith counseled us so many times. . . .

At Iowa City we secured handcarts, and packing in our few belongings, we started on the long journey to Zion. We left Iowa City July 15, 1856, with 120 handcarts and six wagons. Mrs. Bain and her daughters and I pulled one cart. The weather was very hot at times and we suffered considerably, but we got along fine for some time compared with what came to us later. . . . Our food now began to run short, and we were put on short rations. We did not have flour to make bread and made a sort of gruel which we had to live on from day to day. We had a terrible time. For two days we had a soda cracker each. Captain Willie tried to encourage us, but things looked gloomy indeed. Deaths were occurring nearly every day. It began to snow, and at night we had to sweep the snow away to make down our beds. In sorrow and hunger and falling strength we tugged at our handcarts, hardly able to get them up the little hills.

One day [October 19] we saw a dust [cloud] coming towards us from the west. It was a lone horseman. It proved to be Brother Wheelock. He called to us and told us help was near. He stood by and said how he never expected to see brethren and sisters in such a condition as we were. Tears ran down his cheeks as he spoke to us and encouraged us, saying help would reach us [soon], and we should have plenty to eat.

Help did come in the shape of several wagonloads of provisions, clothing, etc. We were allowed one pound of flour in the morning and the same in the evening. The wagons went on to help the Martin company, which was behind us. Other help came to us as we went on, but the [weather turned] very cold, and many froze their feet, and many others died. The Lord blessed our little band, the widow Bain, her daughters, and I. We suffered hunger, thirst, and fatigue, but were well, and none of us froze our feet. We all came through safe and sound. We started with about 500 souls, and 66 died on the journey.

—Euphemia Mitchell, emigrated from Scotland aboard the *Thornton* before joining the Willie handcart company (Allphin, *Tell My Story, Too*, 75–76; see also 127–29, 410)

About three miles on this side of Green River, as I was walking ahead of the train, leading my little brother of six and encouraging him along by telling him stories of what he would get when we arrived at the valley, he said, "When we get to that creek, I wish we could see our brother, Rob." I said, "Come along, maybe we will when we get to the top of the bank." When we arrived at the top of the bank and looked down, we saw a wagon with just one yoke of oxen on. We had never seen the like before, so we waited on the summit until they should pass. The man stared at us, and as his team came beside us, he yelled "Whoa" to the oxen. It was then we knew him. He jumped off the wagon and caught his sisters in his arms as they came up with the cart. ***How we all wept with joy!*** The cart was then tied behind the wagon. Little Alex climbed into the wagon as happy as a prince instead of a poor tired child.

—Elizabeth Smith, emigrated from Scotland aboard the *Thornton* before joining the Willie handcart company (Allphin, *Tell My Story, Too*, 410)

HOW WE ALL WEPT WITH JOY!

We Knew Him © Julie Rogers

When we arrived at those old log cabins, my feet were found to be frozen very badly. While there, they were thawed out and turned black. The rest of the way I was taken care of by kind friends; all was done that was possible under the circumstances, but my feet both dropped off before we got to the city, which was in December, if I remember correctly. My legs were amputated above the ankles, and then at the knees. My two brothers had reached Salt Lake City in November. How well do I remember our meeting. I told them not to cry so, for I would have my feet again when I got to heaven. I have walked on my knees for forty years; during that time I have had three operations performed at the knees, the last one by Dr. Seymour B. Young, a young man, a year ago last November. I was married in 1868 [to Elijah Parsons]. I am the mother of seven children, four sons and three daughters, five of whom are now living.

—Maren Kjirstine Johansen (Mary C. Johnson Parsons), emigrated from Denmark before joining the Hunt wagon company (Deseret Evening News, June 29, 1897, 8; Allphin, *Tell My Story, Too*, 386)

My dear children, we have suffered beyond anything you can imagine. We have seen our comrades weaken and die and be buried in trenches of snow. But in all this suffering we have come face to face with God. It was God who upheld us when our weary bodies would have given up the ghost. It was God who preserved Thisbe to us when it seemed that she would never live. Yes, my children, for the first time in my life I know God. ***I know that He hears our prayers, and that in His wisdom all is for the best.***

—Elizabeth Georgiana Quilley Read, emigrated from England aboard the *Horizon* before joining the Martin handcart company (Allphin, *Tell My Story, Too*, 294)

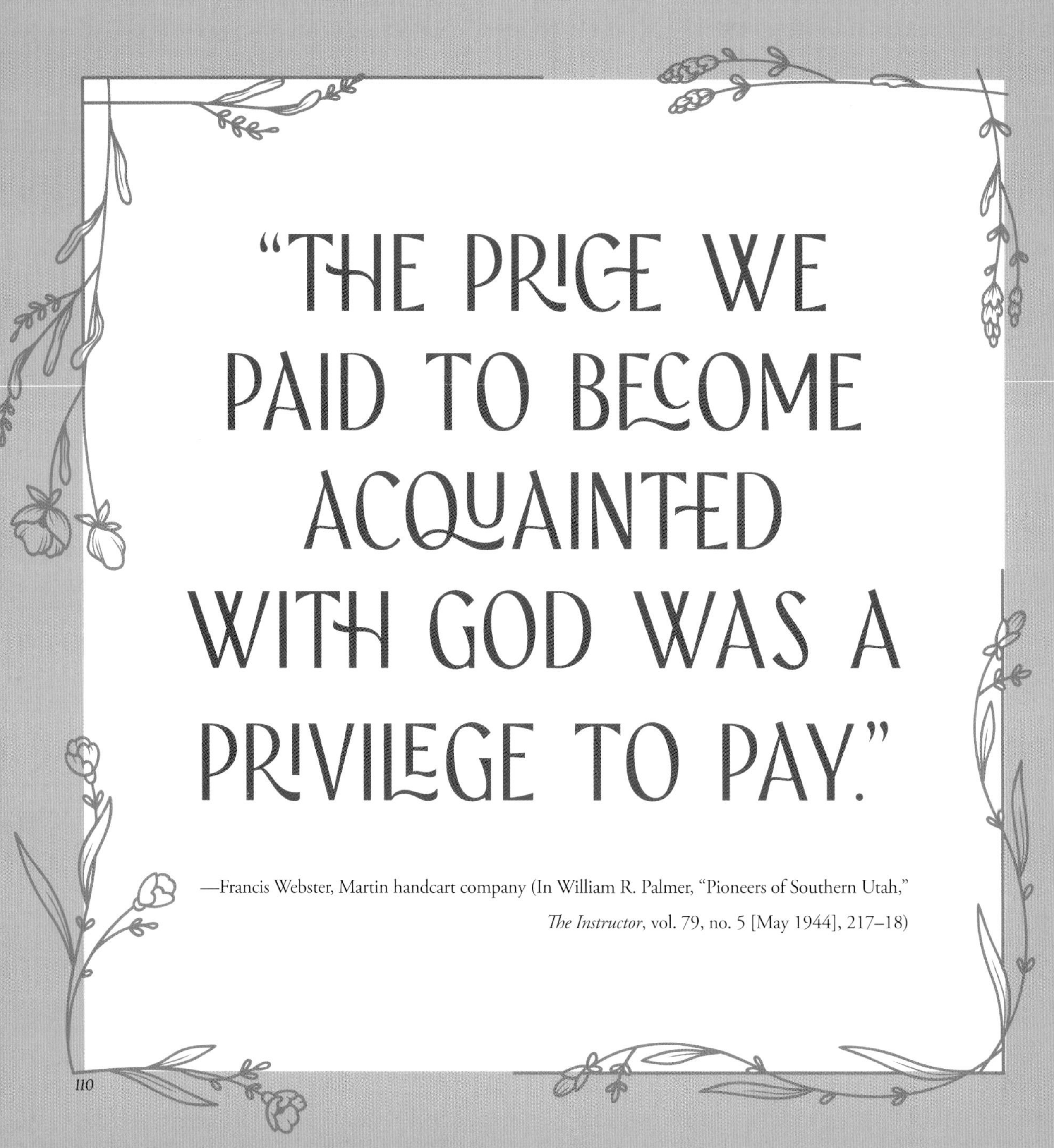

"THE PRICE WE PAID TO BECOME ACQUAINTED WITH GOD WAS A PRIVILEGE TO PAY."

—Francis Webster, Martin handcart company (In William R. Palmer, "Pioneers of Southern Utah," *The Instructor*, vol. 79, no. 5 [May 1944], 217–18)